A
HearT
TO
SerVE

Serving The Gift & Ministry of God

REGINALD EZELL

Contents

Foreword

First, I want to explain something to you. Before you read this book, you must make a quality decision that you are going to take this information and get a working revelation of it. You must meditate on it, digest it and get it into your heart. You must activate it by putting it to practical use. If you do not decide to do this up-front, it won't benefit you to read any further. However, if you are able to prove to yourself that this information both bears witness to your spirit and is indeed substantiated in God's Word, then I encourage you to apply it to your life. I know it will help you in your calling, help you better serve your pastor, your church, and help you better understand how the Body of Christ fits together.

*This book is dedicated to my pastor
and friend Dr. Creflo A. Dollar. Jr.
In appreciation for his godly leadership and
for allowing me to operate in my calling as a servant.
This inspired me to write this book.*

Preface

The first thing you need to do is to start thinking big. You can never go by what you see or by what you do not see. You must realize that it is God's will to have a big church.

The Bible says in Job 8:7, "Though thy beginning was small, yet thy latter end should greatly increase." This means that God is a God of increase. He wants His people to do great things in the earth. God wants big churches. Think of it this way. The bigger your church becomes the fewer souls going to hell. God has called your church to change this world for His glory. Therefore, do not prevent God from expanding your existing ministry. And, do not ever do anything that hinders the vision that God has given to your pastor.

Your church could represent the arms of the Body of Christ, while the Ministry of Helps within your church could be the hands. There are different fingers attached to the hands, and one of them may represent the calling that God has placed on your life. The only question is, "Are you willing to do your part, whatever it takes, to help fulfill God's calling on your life?"

My pastor once talked about putting oneself in the right position just like a pitcher and a catcher in a baseball game. The pitcher is not going to throw the ball unless the catcher gets in a position to receive it. In your church if you do not put yourself and your calling in position to receive the blessings of God, then God can not pitch to you.

You must also realize that you have a key part to play in the assignment that God has given to your church. There are a lot of people who are depending on you to be obedient to your calling whether it is singing, working as a sound technician, ushering, or being a personal aide to your pastor. Regardless of where you work in the church, God has called you to be the best that you can be for Him. Remember, your calling is not based on your ability: it is based on allowing God to work through you.

It is my sincere desire that after you read this book, you will be motivated to seek God for your part in His plan for your church, because you want to one day hear God say to You:—"My good and faithful servant, well done . . ."

Chapter 1

The Purpose of the Ministry of Helps

What Part Do You Play?

And God hath set some in the church, first apostles, secondarily prophets, thirdly teacher, after that miracles, then gifts of healings, helps, governments, diversities of tongues"

I CORINTHIANS 12:28

This scripture identifies the Ministry of Helps as a supernatural ministry. It is listed among such things as miracles and healings. It is a gift that God has set in the church like a concrete pillar. It is like a strong column that God has placed in the church so that it can function properly.

You may think that you only go to church to worship God; however, you also got to be trained and taught the ways of God, so that you can learn how to become an effective witness outside of your church.

You have a purpose in your church. You should not be there just because you have some free time during the week. You should understand that you need to be there because God has something he wants you to do for Him. In the same way God called your pastor to the pulpit, He has called you to do something special for His Kingdom. Your calling begins by understanding how you relate to the divine order that God has established in the church.

"And he gave some, apostles: and some, prophets: and some, evangelists: and some, pastors and teachers . . ."

EPHESIANS 4:11

In every church, God has appointed one man to oversee the sheep, or to teach and train His people. Everyone else at the church has been called to serve this man and do the work within the ministry.

If you have been called to the Ministry of Helps, then you should be giving some type of assistance, directly or indirectly, to the man that God has appointed as true overseer. If you are not helping in some way, not supporting your pastor totally in his work, then you are causing a problem within your church. If you feel that you have indeed been called to attend and support your church, you should not be a problem; you should be an asset. You should be assisting your pastor and not hindering him or the work that God has called him to.

When God began to reveal to me that everyone in the church is to support the pastor, I saw my responsibilities clearly. God's instructions were simple. I was to support my pastor wholeheartedly.

You need to have this same attitude if you desire to walk in God's best. If you are attending a church (which you should be doing), you must decide that you will serve your pastor by working somewhere within the church. If you agree to do this, then God will start moving you toward your ultimate calling.

When I first started working at my church, I knew that God had called me to personally serve my pastor. I was to become a Pastor's Personal Aide, or a P.P.A. I knew that God had called me to become like Joshua was to Moses; Elisha was to Elijah and the armor bearer was to Jonathan. However, at the time I began to serve at my church; my pastor did not need me to be his P.P.A at that time; but God had already given me a revelation on servanthood, I simply found a need and met it. I found out that my pastor needed an Audio Technician; so I became one.

God had already given me a heart to serve this man: however, when I became a technician, I did not have an angel tell me to do it. God did not speak to me from a burning bush and tell me there was a need in this department; I simply found a need and met it. This is what a servant does: they are willing to do whatever needs to be done.

Today, in my office, there is a plaque which reads "Assistant Technician." I became a technician because that is what my pastor needed me to do at the time. What does your pastor need you to be? If there are not any "openings" in the area in which you feel you are called to serve, are you still willing to do your part and serve anyway? That means serving anywhere until the opening in the area that you believe you are called to serve becomes available.

Born Again To Serve

You have to understand that if you are born-again, you have been called to be a servant of God. This is your whole purpose for existence. This is your whole reason for living, to serve Him and His purpose. You are not your own anymore. Furthermore, you need to get a clear understanding of why you are living in this day and time. After all, you could have been born in another generation; but, because of God's reasons you are living in this day and time. You need to find out what that purpose is so that you can fulfill it. This is important because your purpose is your calling. It is the very reason you live and breathe.

"But now being made free from sin, and become servants of God, ye have your fruit unto holiness, and the end everlasting life."

ROMANS 6:22

This scripture reveals that when you accept Jesus, you are made free from sin. Once you become free from sin, you automatically become a servant of God. This comes together as a package deal. You can not have one without the other. In other words, becoming free from sin translates into servanthood.

> *"Let every man abide in the same calling wherein he was called . . ."*
> *"Art thou called being a servant? Care not for it: but if thou mayest be made free, use it rather."*
> *"For he that is called in the Lord, being a servant, is the Lord's freeman: likewise also he that is called, being free, is Christ's servant."*

> I CORINTHIANS 7:20-22

These verses further support the calling into servanthood, once you have been made free from sin. It is critical that you understand this point. You must know that you were not created and born-again just to continue living life the way you desire, without contributing to the Kingdom. God sent His Son for you. Jesus gave up his life so that you could be made free from sin and live in eternity with Him. Now, you must begin to serve Him.

> *"Ye are bought with a price; be not ye the servants of men.*

> I CORINTHIANS 7:23

Jesus paid a price for you. You are not your own. If you buy something, it belongs to you, right? If you buy a car, for example, you would want to get the full use out of that car seven days a week, not just on Sundays. So it is with God. He bought you and when you accepted Jesus, you accepted His price. This especially applies to everyone who claims to be born-again, but it also says that they are fire baptized and filled with the Holy Spirit. If you have said that God paid the price for you, then you must let Him have your life. Let Him run your life. Let Him do with your life whatever he wants to do with it. Allow Him to use you for His Glory. If you ever want to fulfill your calling, you must be willing to become a technician.

Called To a Specific Work

"Brethren, let every man, wherein he is called, therein abide with God.

I CORINTHIANS 7:24

God has called you to do something, no matter who you are and even if you do not think you have any talents. God has called you to do a specific work. If you are having a hard time hearing from God, maybe you are in the wrong place. You are probably seeking the wrong sign. In order to find out what He has called you to do, you need to get in a position to receive His instructions. To hear from God personally about your calling, read His Word. In the pages of His Word is where He is waiting to speak to you. He will meet you there and is ready to give you precise information.

A lot of people have problems fulfilling their calling because they do not know how to make it happen. They know "up-front" what they are supposed to be doing but they do not know which steps to take to do it. It may be the same way with you and your calling. You may even have some specific directions, but you are not sure how to follow them.

God is faithful to take care of those He has called. If you will get into His Word, He will give you a printed road map with all the key landmarks identified. He will meet you at every intersection and direct you to the fullness of your calling.

Remember, you are not waiting on Him to call you. He has already done that. He is waiting on you to find your calling. We should not be waiting for Jesus to make His enemies His footstool. The feet are attached to the body; and we are the feet attached to the

Body of Christ. Until each member of the Body fulfills their calling, this scripture goes unfulfilled.

My pastor, Dr. Creflo Dollar, ministers and teaches on God's purpose for the anointing. One of the things that he frequently says is that the anointing only operates correctly when you are in the right place. When you are where you are supposed to be, then and only then is the anointing present to give you results . . . sweatlessly.

However, if you are constantly struggling to do what you know God has called you to do—and for some reason it is not working—you may need to dig deeper into God's Word to find out where you went wrong. Begin by examining yourself to see if you are really on the right track, or if you need to make some adjustments.

"There is one body, and one spirit, even as ye are called in one hope of your calling;"

EPHESIANS 4:4

When God calls people, He puts a calling on their lives that is bigger than they can ever accomplish on their own. That is why it is so important that you put your trust in Him. He will give you something that will take both you and Him to make it happen.

The only hope that you have in walking in the fullness of your calling is in Him. If He is not motivating your actions; if He is not governing what you do; if He is not directing your footsteps, then you will not be successful in your calling. You must understand this: to be successful in the things of God, you have got to put Him where He needs to be in your life.

God's Work is not About You
"Faithful is he that calleth you, who also will do it."

I THESSALONIANS 5:24

God's work is God's work. It is not about you. It never has been and it never will be. If He called you to do it, then He is going to do it through you, because it is all about Him. When I pray, I confess that "there is no lack in me", because I abide in Him. I stand on the Word that promises, "I can do all things through Christ the Anointed One." You should already know that you can not be an effective servant without having the power of the Holy Spirit helping you do the work.

Do you realize that when you truly became born-again, you received His ability? You received His anointing. You received everything that it takes to accomplish and to fulfill the calling upon your life when you became filled with His Spirit.

Chapter 2

Doing the Right Work Right

Understanding Authority

"Let every soul be subject unto the higher powers. For there is no power but of God: the powers that be are ordained of God.

Whosoever therefore resisteth the power, resisteth the ordinance of God: and they that resist shall receive to themselves damnation".

ROMANS 13: 1-2

The word "servant" is frequently defined as one who is under another's authority. A servant is one who serves or ministers to someone else. If you have been called to be a servant, then you have been called to serve God by serving man. You have been called to obey and to minister to someone else's needs. If you are called to serve a particular pastor, then any act that you do is under the authority of his ministry. You should not ever pursue your own plans, your own purposes, or your own agenda. As a servant, you must conform to the needs of the ministry that you have been called to serve.

"And he gave some, apostles; and some, prophets: and some evangelists: and some, pastors and teachers; For the perfecting of the saints, for the work of the ministry, for the edifying of the body of Christ: Till we all come in the unity of the faith, and of the knowledge of the Son of God, unto a perfect man, unto the measure of the stature of the fullness of Christ:"

EPHESIANS 4: 11-13

Your entire goal as a servant and a member of your church is to get into the right place. The pastor's job is to perfect the saints by teaching the Word, so you can do the work of the ministry; then the entire Body of Christ will be edified. This is God's divine order. All authority is ordained by God. His Word reveals this to us.

Let us look at what you should understand thus far. You know you have been called to serve. You know to get into position to hear from God on you calling by reading His Word. You know that you have been made free from sin, so fulfilling your calling is your reasonable service.

A servant has got to be willing to serve somebody. A servant must recognize the authority that has been pre-established in the church. If you are in the Ministry of Helps, you must submit to your pastor and to the leadership within you church. You must do this in the same way that you desire to submit to God's authority.

My pastor often tells a story about a little boy named Johnny, who wanted to go out and play. His parents told him to sit down and do his homework. He sat down but he was very angry about it. In reality, because of his attitude, he was sitting down on the outside, but on the inside he was outside playing. Unfortunately, a lot of people who are called to be servants have the same attitude as Johnny.

Becoming submissive is your own decision. Nobody can make you do it. Your pastor can not make you and God will not make you. You must make up your own mind to become submissive according to God's Word.

*"Who hath saved us, and called us with a holy calling,
not according to our works, but according to his own purpose
and grace, which was given us in Christ Jesus before the world
began . . ."*

II TIMOTHY 1:9

The Holy Calling

Again, He has saved you and called you. The reason that He saved you is He expects a work out of you. He has saved you and called you to a "Holy Calling". In God's Word a "Holy calling" means you belong to God, such as the Holy tithe and the Holy temple. The "Holy calling" belongs to God. He called you, but you belong to Him. He is expecting you to do with it what He wants you to do.

A "Holy calling" is not reflected by your works. You can be busy working and not fulfill your calling. This bears repeating. You can be busy working and not fulfill your calling. This is proven in the above scripture. Think of how frightening it would be to stand in front of the almighty God and hear Him say, "Depart from me, I never knew you." You are called "according to His purpose and grace". God does not expect you to perform your work. He expects you to work His purpose.

Proving God's Word

*"But let every man prove his own work, and then shall he
have rejoicing in himself alone, and not in another."*

GALATIANS 6:4

To determine whether you are working right, one might say "the proof is in the pudding". If you are indeed doing the right work, then it will be done under the anointing of God. This proves that the work is of God. However, if you are working and no one is being affected, or there is no evidence of righteous fruit, you are not proving the Word. But when it is God's work, expect lives to change. If you are in the right position, the anointing will speak for itself.

You rejoice in yourself, not because of who you are, but whose you are. You should not rejoice because of yourself and your own ability, but because He lives in you and gives you the ability. I thank God for Him being a part of my life. I thank God for His power which operates through me. I recognize that without Him, I can not fulfill my calling. However, because I recognize who He is, I can rejoice when I lay my hands on the sick and see them recover. This is because I understand that I am an instrument of God; one that He uses for His will and purpose. When you can prove your calling like this, you will have the right to rejoice too!

"For every man shall bear his own burden."

GALATIANS 6:5

This scripture does not refer to a burden that God has placed on you. It refers to the calling on your life, and the accountability that comes with it. One day you must stand before God and you will be judged on your life's work. You will have to give an account of what you did with what He called you to do.

In other words, you can do a lot of good works on this earth, but, if God did not call you to do the work, it will not count and your work would have been in vain.

Working outside of your calling is like giving an offering without paying your tithes. You can give all the offerings you want, but unless you also give your tithes, the offering will not count. It is not righteous. Until you start fulfilling the call upon your life, the work that you do does not matter, it is your work. This is why it is so important that you get yourself in a position to hear from God, so that you can start moving in Him.

Get Up and Get Moving

*"Whatsoever thy hand findeth to do, do it with thy might;
for there is no work, nor device, nor knowledge, nor wisdom, in
the grave, whither thou goest."*

ECCLESIASTES 9:10

Perhaps you do not know what God has called you to do, so you justify this as the reason for doing nothing. However, this is the point at which you need to start doing something—whatever your hands find to do—so that God can begin to direct your steps. Once you start moving and doing things, He will start leading you. As you continue to seek His calling upon your life, He will begin to minister to your heart. When you start asking, seeking and knocking, He will reveal His divine plan for your life.

You know that God is watching you. You know that you will give an answer for everything that you do. You know that you are going to give an account of how well you perform what He has called you to do. So why are you waiting? Get busy moving towards your calling.

*"Servants, obey in all things your masters according
to the flesh; not with eye service, as men pleasers; but in
singleness of heart, fearing God:"*

COLOSSIANS 3:22

Your servanthood goes well beyond your service in the church. This is often a problem for believers. For some reason, too many Christians do not want to keep their "servant's attitude" outside of the church. Serving is not hard when the boss is looking. These "men pleasers" forget that God is watching all the time.

You need to be consistent in your serving, because of God, because you recognize you are doing the work of your Father, and because you know you are representing God and He is watching you. Once you learn to work this way, you learn to please your Father and you will not care who sees you working. You know that your Father sees in secret and rewards openly.

"Knowing that of the Lord ye shall receive the reward of the inheritance: for ye serve the Lord Christ."

COLOSSIANS 3:24

Let us go back over some basics. You get saved; you start working by first serving somewhere in the church. You get yourself in a position to hear from God. Once you start moving in your calling, you start reaping the fruit of your labor. Then, after you complete your life's work, you receive everlasting life. You recognize that this is eternal. You are working on your eternal life through your servanthood on this earth. The bonus is that in the midst of working, you reap the fruit of God's goodness. Think about it all this way, when you choose to be obedient to your calling, you will be blessed in this world and the world to come.

Recognize Your Call

I have known Pastor Creflo A. Dollar, Jr. for a long time. I met him before World Changers Ministries began. I even received an invitation to attend the first church service. I knew that God had called me to do something mighty in the ministry and I was searching for the right church home.

The first time I went to WORLD CHANGERS MINISTRIES, in College Park, Georgia, as I listened to Pastor Creflo Dollar preaching, I remember saying out loud, "This is it!" "This is good!" I remember vividly, because people around me kept telling me to "hush", but I was so absorbed in the message that I did not realize what I was doing.

It was at this time that God spoke to my heart and said, "You see that man? I want you to be whatever he needs you to be. This is what I have called you to do. At that time, Pastor Dollar already had a person serving him. It was not likely that I was going to get the opportunity to become his personal aide too soon, but I remembered what God told me when he said to "be whatever he needs you to be."

God had spoken to me specifically. As time went on, He started revealing more and more to me about my call. I dug deeper and deeper into His Word, and started getting busier and busier about the things of God for my life.

I did not start out doing everything at once for my pastor. I recognized that Pastor had a need for a technician, so I became a technician. The ministry was growing rapidly, and as time continued my responsibilities increased. I first, however, had to prove my diligence as a technician. God continued to reveal His will to me and in due season I was elevated to be Pastor's primary personal aide.

God desires to speak to you also. He does not want you to be in the dark concerning His call for your life, but you must be in proper position to hear. You must get busy doing the work of the ministry. I have always said, whatever your hands find to do, do it! This will help you hear the voice of God concerning His will for your life.

Do not Become Distracted

When you start moving in the things of God, persecution will come. You must understand why this happens. It comes to take your focus off of what God has called you to do.

For example, how can sickness come when you know God's promises on healing? It is a distraction. Satan wants you to pay more attention to cold symptoms than to God's Word. Most of the time trouble and tribulation will cease a lot quicker if you do not react to it.

We all know that Satan comes to kill, to steal, and to destroy. But Satan can not do anymore than you allow him to do. His purpose in your life is to be a distraction. When God desires to bless you, no man on earth, or Satan in Hell—can stop your blessing. You are the only one who can stop it. When you allow Satan to get you focused on your problems rather than on the things of God, you hinder your blessings. Do not allow Satan to become a distraction. Always remember that whatever Satan says is a lie.

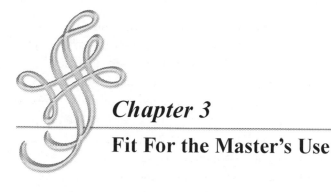

Chapter 3

Fit For the Master's Use

What Price will you pay?

> *"He that is faithful in that which is least is faithful also in much: and he that is unjust in the least is unjust also in much."*

LUKE 16:10

Before I joined World Changers and became involved with the P.P.A.'s, I cleaned bathrooms for my former employer. I used a toothbrush to scrub between the bathroom tiles. When I left that job, I was one of the highest paid supervisors in the company. Why? It was because I knew how to pay attention to detail; I had the heart of Abraham. I was willing to do whatever it would take to please my employer, thus pleasing my Master. God knew everything that Abraham was willing to do with Isaac even before He asked him to do it. God is sovereign. He knows what you can do and what you will do in order to fulfill His call on your life. All God is waiting for is for you to find out what you are willing to do. He is waiting for you to pay attention to detail. When you agree to do the "not so glorious jobs", such as sweeping floors or cleaning bathrooms it really demonstrates your faithfulness to God.

Become a Yielded Vessel

Ironically, you do not have to put pressure on yourself to receive or work within your call. In fact, once you are a servant of God, you do not ever need to put a lot of pressure on yourself to do anything. All you need to do is to learn to go to God for help and guidance. It will all be presented to you if you put pressure on God and His Word. He will reveal His plan for your life, if you become a yielded vessel.

Think of it this way. You know that God does not need your money. The Word says that He already owns everything. The only thing that He really needs is a vessel to channel His money through. He wants to give you money, so He can accomplish His purpose.

Do you understand? Or, are you continuing to hold onto your money thinking that what you have belongs to you? If you do this, then you will be forever limited to your supply of money. But, if you allow yourself to be a vessel through which God can channel His money, then all of your needs and His needs through you are going to be met. So it is with your call. He completely owns it. All you need to become is a yielded and willing vessel so God can channel whatever He wants through you. The same thing applies with your money, when you put your confidence in God and His work, you will end-up becoming the beneficiary.

Getting In Shape

How far should you go with God. Should you become radical in your servanthood? Yes! There should not be a limit to your commitment. You should be willing to become extremely disciplined, so that you can fulfill the call of God on your life.

How far do you go to establish disciplined procedures? It takes planning, training and teaching. Let me tell you what I did with my P.P.A.s. One of their responsibilities was to make sure the entire church was cleaned after each service. Services were scheduled every Wednesday and Friday night. Pastor feels that he can take more time to minister the Word, so usually Friday night cleaning is done very late. However, no matter how late they remained on Friday night, they were expected to attend a 7:00 a.m. meeting every Saturday morning. I could have scheduled the meeting later, but I wanted to see where their hearts were. All of this was done because I needed to know if they were able to discipline their flesh enough to get up and get going. We had a twofold meeting on Saturday. We started out in a classroom setting where they received instructions and information. The second half of the meeting was based on discipline and exercise. I guess you may ask, "Why exercise?" It is because our pastor stays in good physical condition so that God can work and use him. If the P.P.A.'s are going to aid and assist the pastor, they also need to be in good physical condition. However, if they are lazy—like the disciples were when Jesus prayed—then they are not going to be able to help much.

I once told one of my P.P.A.s, "When I tell you to run, it is not to get you in good condition, but it is to show you what kind of condition you are already in." Those that could not keep up got the message.

To what extreme do you take servanthood? How far do you take it, especially in leadership? In leadership, you are responsible for training. It is a necessity that you invest quality time. I do admit that a lot of times I felt too tired to go to church or to do anything for my pastor. I had to drive 45 minutes just to get there. But, I did it anyway, because I had to set a good example for the leadership in the Ministry of Helps and also for the P.P.A.'s.

As a servant of God, you have to set the same example. How far do you take this type of discipline? You take it all the way.

Making It Work

When you are training people, such as P.P.A.'s, you will need to put the "qualifying rules" down on paper in black and white. They will need to know what is expected of them. By doing this, you never disqualify them from their position; they disqualify themselves. You establish the guidelines; it is up to them to obey the rules. When they do not obey, they need to understand that there will be consequences.

Rules and procedural manuals will become even more important as your ministry grows. People will need to know the consequences for not showing up on time for a meeting or missing a church service. They need to know that. Why, is irrelevant"—why they were late or why they missed church does not negate the consequences. How far do you take it? You take it all the way if you want your ministry to run in excellence.

How extreme do you take the things that God has called you to do? For me and my calling, I take everything personally. My calling was to serve my pastor and to make things run smooth for him. I took my job very seriously.

At World Changers church, all of the P.P.A.'s were required to have a job outside of the ministry. We did not want any freeloaders. The candidates were required to furnish all kinds of information, including their current supervisor's name. I wanted them to feel accountable. I also needed to know if the person had ever served in another department at the church. I certainly did not want someone else's headache. The candidate had to identify all family members who also attended the church. I wanted to check this person out.

A lot of people use work as an excuse to not serve in the church. However, if someone was applying for the position of P.P.A. and worked the night shift, they soon learned that there was work to be done during the day at the church. How far do you take your calling? I hope you take it all the way.

As a born-again believer, you should be the best employee that your employer has. Why? You should be better equipped than non-believers in your work place, because you have the Holy Spirit living on the inside of you, which goes beyond your knowledge and your ability. I would often call my P.P.A.'s supervisor to find out what kind of employee they were. If they can not work well in the world, they are not going to make a good servant in the church. If he is causing problems at work, they will cause problems in the church too.

You Need a Vision

The Bible says "Without a vision, the people perish", (Proverb 29:18). This verse of scripture explains the importance of having a manual for your department. It is vitally important that everyone understand clearly what their responsibilities are. If they do not know the vision and purpose of their job, more than likely they will mess up.

I often use the example of the War of Independence. The Englishmen were well-trained, but they did not know why they were fighting. All they knew was that they were fighting because the Monarch ordered it. But the colonies, the Americans, were fighting for independence.

They knew their purpose, because they had a vision of freedom. I believe this is why they won. It works the same way in servanthood. If people know why they are serving, they are more motivated to do a good job.

They also need to know the way God demands work to be done, and that they will be held accountable for their job. They need to see the right attitude demonstrated from the leadership down, or from the top down. Anything, from the top down is the solution. Anything from the bottom up is a revolution.

God has set His divine order for everything. God is first, the pastor is second, and the ministry is third. Before miracles can take place, this order has to be established. For example, when Jesus fed the multitude He first established order.

The church also needs to have an established order and flow chart. For example, the ushers need to know who to seat first and who to seat next. People called to the music ministry need to understand their purpose. They need to know that they do not just sing because they sound good. They need to be in line with the pastor and his call; they should sing songs that are in line with his message for the day. Choirs need to realize their part in preparing the hearts of the congregation to receive the Word of God.

Every department needs an established order. All of this takes careful planning and a lot of prayer by the leadership. Leadership must pray and ask God to give the people wisdom and understanding on how to fulfill their call.

Chapter 4

The Heart to Serve

Knowing Your Pastor

G od placed in my heart the desire to serve my pastor. Without compromise, my purpose was to allow him to spend quality time with God. He should not have concern for the work of the ministry. My heart became like my pastor's through praying for him, observing him, and serving him. If you are called to be a P.P.A., this is one way you can get the heart of your pastor.

As a P.P.A., one of the most valuable qualities you should possess is the ability to listen, especially during casual conversation with your pastor. If it is not in a business-type setting, you may not think that what he says is really important. However, those things that are told in casual conversation often represent the heart of the individual. They must also be acted upon.

When you carry out his actual desires—under the direction of the Holy Spirit—it helps to accomplish the vision that God Has given your pastor for the ministry.

A lot of people get into trouble because they think something should be done differently from what their pastor wants. You need to realize, it is not your calling. It is not your vision, so do not try to run it. Support him until God blesses you with your own ministry. If you are not sticking to the vision of your pastor, you are out of order. Remember, he is ultimately responsible before God.

You know you are effectively serving your pastor when you are able to respond to situations the same way he would. For example, in a counseling session, the person should get the same answers from you that he would receive from your pastor. When your pastor knows that he can rely on you like this—to give his same answers—he should be able to cut his counseling sessions in half.

Every pastor needs to know that he has a group of men in his ministry who are willing to do anything and everything to make it work, to accomplish the vision that God has given him for the church. Oneness does not begin with a corporate body getting together and deciding what they are going to do. Oneness begins with an individual's decision to make it work, to make somebody else's vision a reality. If you have not made this decision, you need to make it. Your pastor needs to know if he can not get in touch with anybody else, he can call on you and you will come through.

Tested on the Commitment

When I was working at a certain company, my boss knew that if my pastor called and needed me, I was leaving my job. My boss knew I was committed to my church and my pastor. He would not have permitted me to leave if I had not been an outstanding employee.

If you claim to be committed to serving your pastor, you will be tested on that commitment. If you have ever opened your mouth and said "Pastor, you can call on me," the call is going to come through. Are you prepared to answer it? He needs to know you are willing to do whatever needs to be done, regardless of how uncomfortable the task may be. If you are willing to serve your pastor in this way, you must know that you are going to have to put your comfort level aside. At times, you are even going to have to be more concerned about how comfortable he is, rather than how bone-tired you are.

I have had many calls from my pastor at three o'clock in the morning. You will be called to do things that may not be to comfortable for you to do. Once my pastor called and asked me to go to the hospital and pray for a little boy who had been run over by a car. You may find this part of the job too uncomfortable. You may think that this is the pastor's job. But as a servant of God, if he needs you to do it, then you need to do it.

The little boy went on to be with the Lord. It was a rough situation for me, but I had to be strong for the mom and dad. We prayed and believed God for comfort. This was a call I had to answer. Could you answer a call like this? Your pastor needs to know!

There were a couple of occasions when my pastor called me at 2:00 a.m. and informed me some members were in jail. He asked me to go and get them. I had to get up and go. Could you answer a call like this one? Could you get out of bed regardless of how tired you are? Will you prove yourself faithful to your pastor and to your call?

The Right Attitude

P.P.A.'s are not just a group of people. To really become a P.P.A., you need a certain attitude, one that is able to carry on the spirit of the ministry. There was a P.P.A. that served in the Tape Ministry who had the right attitude. What ever he did, he did it right the first time and every time.

If you really want to be an effective Personal Aide to your pastor, make sure that the area you serve in does not become a headache for your pastor. Do the work with the right attitude. Anybody can claim to be a P.P.A., but it is not about the title. It is about serving the man of God—SO THAT HE DOES NOT HAVE TO BE CONCERNED ABOUT WHAT YOU HAVE BEEN CALLED TO DO. You must become the least of his troubles.

If you have been called to serve your pastor, do not wait constantly for someone else to do your work. Just do it, no matter what it takes. When you have the right attitude, and you are able to do the work, it further proves your calling.

When you are called to the Ministry of Helps, you should also have the heart of a P.P.A. The other P.P.A.'s should not have to serve and support you. You should be self-sufficient. But, unfortunately, too many people within the church often rely on others to do their jobs.

I can remember when my pastor once said, the parking lot attendants are not doing what they are supposed to do, Reginald, get some guys out there." I replied, "Yes Sir." I took care of it. Once, he said, "The Children's Ministry is not adequately staffed. Reginald, get some people over there." I replied, "Yes Sir." And I handled it. This happened time and time again. Each time, I had one standard answer, "Yes Sir." And, I did whatever needed to be done. As his personal aide, this was my job. I had to be willing to step-in when another department failed. And, yes, it was touchy at times, especially when I had to correct areas that other people perceived were their "exclusive" responsibility. But, I had to do it anyway, because I was called to serve my pastor.

Unquestionable Integrity

A bishop then must be blameless, the husband of one wife, vigilant, sober, of good behavior, given to hospitality, apt to teach;"

I TIMOTHY 3:2

"But a lover of hospitality, a lover of good men, sober, just, holy, temperate;"

TITUS 1:8

There should be qualifications for becoming a P.P.A. at any church. The primary one is to be blameless, and have unquestionable integrity. A P.P.A. must be an excellent example to the flock. In addition, a P.P.A. must meet all of the following criteria:

Good Behavior—Modest, orderly, disciplined and well-behaved.
Vigilant—Wide awake, watchful, not careless or carefree.

Temperate—Slow to anger, under control, self-disciplined.

Sober—Discrete, not given to wine, sound-minded, stable.

Just—Right standing with God and people, giver of good reports.

Lover of Good—Righteous and peaceful, lover of the good things of God.

Patient—Tolerant of others, calm.

Not covetous or Quarrelsome—Cooperative, not a brawler, not greedy.

In addition, a P.P.A. must be a good steward over all of the things of God. They must recognize that they are called to manage God's household and that they are employed by God to manage His affairs.

> *"Let every soul be subject unto the higher Powers. For there is no power but of God: the powers that be are ordained of God."*
>
> *"Whosoever therefore resisteth the power, resisteth the ordinance of God: and they that resist shall receive to themselves damnation."*

ROMANS 13: 1-2

A P.P.A. must walk in agreement and in submission to all authority in the church. In order to be a P.P.A., you must settle it in your heart that all authority is established by God. You must make up your mind to submit to this authority the same way you would submit to Jesus.

Display Your Faithfulness

One thing that I really want to stress is "to be strong in the Lord." A true P.P.A. is always displaying a position and attitude of faithfulness. If you are to be successful in serving your pastor, he must sense your victory and joy as a tangible part of your life. This alone can minister to him. It helps your pastor to know that he does not have to "carry" his aides, whether it is physically, mentally, spiritually, or even financially. It is a comfort to your pastor to know that you are where you are supposed to be, so he does not have to "carry" you. You must understand that he can not grow deeper into the things of God, if he constantly has to minister to you. There must come a time when your pastor can reap from the seeds he has sown into your life.

Your pastor also needs to see the manifestation of the Word in your life. This is when you can become a real aide to him, because you have become united in faith. Then, when you come together in prayer—as in touching—you both will know that God will move, because you have become one in agreement.

There are three stages of son-ship. The first stage—The father imparts to the son; Second stage—The son and father are like friends imparting to one another; and the third stage—The son is giving back to the father. This is what you and your pastor should experience. You should be able to identify where you are in the three stages of son-ship with your pastor.

Are you giving back to your spiritual father, or does he still have to feed you? Do you realize that he can not always take care of you? Are you like a 50 year-old man still living with mama? Are you not working but still eating off her table? If you want to help your man of God, you will need to become self-sufficient in God and start giving back to your pastor.

At this point, at a minimum, you should understand that if you are born again, you are called in some way to serve your pastor. But do you realize that there are ways to advance the spirit of a true servant? Let's look at what the Word says will help create excellence in us. Examine your own life as you read these points:

"But he giveth more grace. Wherefore he saith, God Resisteth the Proud, But Giveth Grace Unto the Humble."

JAMES 4:6

25

1. *Free yourself from pride.* Evidence of a prideful spirit is any or all of the following: an independent spirit; refusal to ask God or others for help; afraid to make mistakes; rebellious attitude towards those in authority; a proud countenance; self-centered conversations; intolerant of the mistakes of others; and a bossy attitude. Free yourself of pride. It has no place in a born-again believer's life.

   "He that is slow to anger is better than the mighty; and he that ruleth his spirit than he that taketh a city."

   PROVERB 16:32

2. *Free yourself of anger.* Get rid of any evidence of anger such as: temper-tantrums; hostile reaction to supposed injustice; constantly trying to defend yourself; feeling everyone is picking on you; frustration over unchangeable circumstances; and murmuring and complaining. Free yourself of anger. It can not be part of a servant's life.

   "Having therefore these promises, dearly beloved, let us cleanse ourselves from all filthiness of the flesh and spirit, perfecting holiness in the fear of God."

   II CORINTHIANS 7:1

3. *Free yourself of immorality.* Hard evidence of this spirit include: sensual conversations; reading of impure material; general impurity; improper attitude towards members of the opposite sex; a desire to listen to sensual music; sensual dressing and appearance. Free yourself from immorality. Become holy, set aside, and set apart for God's work.

*"Looking diligently lest any man fail of the grace of God;
lest any root of bitterness springing up trouble you, and thereby
many be defiled;"*

HEBREWS 12:15

4. *Free yourself from bitterness.* Examine your life for evidence
such as: a sarcastic and critical tongue; inability to trust
people; frequent illnesses; a self-pity and a sad countenance.
Do not let bitterness hinder your call to serve in any way.
Get rid of these types of things in your life by constantly
confessing God's Word.

Everything is not going to come easy in your ministry. You have
to do some things on your own, such as praying and fasting. You also
need to fast from the things that cause distractions in your life, such
as TV. Remember, God wants to speak to you, but you need to be in
a position to hear from God for yourself. You must know that you are
called; know that you are appointed to become anointed. When you
know this, then you know you can do anything and everything that
the Lord has for you to do.

For most people, it starts with a choice between the call upon
their life and their material possessions. Which one will it be for you?
The Bible is very clear on this point—you can not serve God and
mammon. You have to make the decision. What is the most important
thing in your life? Is it your wife, your job, your children—or God?

The Couple's Calling

At this point, I want to recognize that God calls women to serve
in very specific areas, just like He calls men. However, for this book,
because the primary focus has been on P.P.A.'s, my comments have
largely been directed towards men. I feel it is important to address
married couples.

When God calls the couple, He calls the man to be the head. There is no way to get around this God ordained authority. Unfortunately, a lot of men have trouble walking in their calling because of their wife. The divine order is that the wife must support the call on her husband's life. If he is called to leave the house in the middle of the night, the wife needs to be understanding. If he is called to leave a birthday party, because a church member has been in an accident, and he needs to go and pray, the wife needs to be understanding. She has to always know that he is serving God—not leaving her. Men, you need to explain your calling to your wife, so she can better understand it and grow with it.

Chapter 5

God's Ultimate Purpose

Equipped to be a Witness

You need to understand that when you are called to a church, you are being prepared to go out into the world. The pastor is the teacher that God has called to direct you and train you so that you can become equipped to go back out into the world and be an effective witness. This is God's ultimate calling for everyone. He wants to prepare you to help get others where they need to be. That is why, as a Christian, you can not be selfish with the Gospel. You can not keep it contained in the four walls of your church. Everything that you have learned—at some point—you will need to share.

The world should want to be like you. If what you are learning is not being used or not being seen in your life, then what you say will not really matter. In essence, if someone sees you living a defeated life, they will not want Christ. You can not go forward in the things of God when you always have to turn around and fix that which is broken. In addition, in order for your pastor to go forward, he needs you to fulfill the call upon your life. You have to go back out into the world and bring others into the church.

It is very important to recognize why you should serve God in this way. I serve because God commanded me to serve Him. I serve

Him because I love Him. The Bible says "If you love God, you will keep His commandments." He is commanding you to serve; do it!

Do not Become Complacent or Too Comfortable

> *"Every way of a man is right in his own eyes: but the Lord pondereth the hearts."*

PROVERBS 21:2

You may be thinking, based on what you have read so far, that you are doing pretty good. Again, I want to tell you that you can do much better. In your own eyes, you may be the best servant in your church. I am telling you, do not get complacent or too comfortable. If you do, you will never be used in a greater way by God.

You should always strive to do better, through Him, and through His strength. You may sometimes think you are too tired to go on. But, I guarantee you that if you were asleep and heard the smoke alarm, you would get up and get moving. What I am saying is that I have learned that a person really does not know what his body is capable of doing unless he is willing to go through God's endurance test.

God will help you to serve. You can always do more. You can learn to put your flesh under subjection to the Spirit of God that resides in you. Then, when God tells you to go another step, you can do it, regardless of what your flesh says. Never let your eyes nor your mind determine your limit. In your own mind, you may think you are all right, but remember God searches the heart. He is searching your heart again and again for the reason you serve . . . or stop serving.

Going Beyond Your limit

"All the ways of a man are clean in his own eyes; but the Lord weigheth the spirits. Commit thy works unto the Lord, and thy thoughts shall be established."

PROVERBS 16: 2-3

How far will you go to serve God? Satan knows your limit, and that is where he will always want you to stop. If you believe there is a limit, then you are always going to reach that limit. But if you determine there is not a limit, then God can take you higher into your calling. He wants to meet you at a point where you are willing to keep going, even when your flesh wants you to stop. God wants you to go beyond your natural ability. Because when you are operating in your natural ability, you are not depending on Him. You are depending on yourself and what you can accomplish. However, if you are willing to move in Him, God will move you forward.

We're living in the last days, and God is expecting you to do something that has never been done before. Each individual has to make up his mind that he is going to be the one that will make a difference. You need to have more confidence in God than you have in anybody else. You have to be willing to pay the price for your calling. Do not expect others to pay it for you. You have got to be diligent. You have got to develop and move in the servant's attitude.

Producing a Perfect Work

"Let a man so account of us. as of the ministers of Christ, and stewards of the mysteries of God."

I CORINTHIANS 4:1

Everything hidden in the heart will be manifested. God is watching your heart in everything that you do. You can look good in

31

the eyes of the brethren, but God knows what is really going on in your heart.

God weighs each man's heart separately. What one man is doing may be all that he is capable of doing. This man is blessed. However, if another man can do more, and he is not doing it, God is not pleased. God judges the ability He puts on the inside of you. He can always see through the masquerade.

> *"A good man out of the good treasure of his heart bringeth forth that which is good: and an evil man out of the evil treasure of his heart bringeth forth that which is evil: for of the abundance of the heart his mouth speaketh."*

LUKE 6:45

If your heart is pure towards God, then your actions and what you produce will be pure. You may not be perfect, but you can produce a perfect work. Think about this. If you allow God to work through you, you can produce a perfect work.

> *"I can do all things through Christ which strengtheneth me."*

PHILIPPIANS 4:13

God will strengthen you to do many things that you could not otherwise do through your imperfect vessel. He will help you all the way because the work is not about you. He just needs a vessel. He will do the work.

A good example of how God works is when we speak in tongues. He will provide the words. He just needs a tongue. Another example is when you lay your hands on the sick. He does the healing. He just needs a pair of hands to use. God always does the work. He just needs a yielded vessel; one that is fit for the master's use.

"But seek ye first the kingdom of God, and his righteousness; and all these things shall be added unto you."

MATTHEW 6:33

In everything that you do, you should be seeking the Kingdom of God and His righteousness. Every action that you take should be for the glory of the Kingdom, not ever for your own edification. God will not accept a selfish act. If the work is about you, God will not accept it.

My pastor once did a teaching entitled: "The Unholy Trinity—Selfishness, Pride and Rebellion." This is the trinity of Satan. He wants to be like the most high God. He wants to exalt his throne above God's. This was his motive. Be careful when you serve. Make sure your motives are pure. Do not ever serve your pastor, hoping he will call attention to your work. If this is why you are serving, God will not be a part of it.

Used For His Glory

"Then he which had received the one talent came and said, Lord, I knew thee that thou art a hard man, reaping where thou hast not sown, and gathering where thou hast not strawed:"
And I was afraid, and went and hid thy talent in the earth: lo, there thou host that is thine."
His lord answered and said unto him, Thou wicked and slothful servant, thou knewest that I reap where I sowed not, and gather where I have not strawed."

MATTHEW 25: 24-26

There are a lot of gifted people within the church that the world has trained. They have natural ability. There is nothing wrong with this. In fact, God wants to use it.

Let me explain what God is saying in this scripture. God does not mind Satan training you. He just wants to use that training for His glory, in His Kingdom. You know that Satan only imitates and perverts things. He can not create anything. If the world has trained you to do something, do not sit on that training. Use it for God. God wants to reap where He did not sow. God wants to reap the benefits from your worldly training.

You have talents that you have developed in the world, but you can not see how, as a believer, you can use them for God. Find out what the original intent was for the talents, because He created them.

Becoming an Effective Servant

"For the gifts and calling of God are without repentance."

ROMANS 11:29

Many people stand on this scripture when they refer to the calling on their life. They never think of the possibility of losing that calling. They do not ever think of it like "repentance means a change of direction." I often say that losing the calling is similar to losing your license due to driving under the influence, or a D.U.I. God blessed you with the car, but because you lost your license, you can not drive it anymore. You never lost the car, just the right to use it.

A lot of people are holding D.U.I's on their calling. They are losing the right to the call because they aren't being faithful to the calling. Yet, they still have the calling. Basically, if this is you, you need to repent for your D.U.I. and get on track with God.

Let us look at how to become an effective servant. This should always be your number one desire. This is another key area that you can improve in. Always desire to do better. There are several things I feel each servant of the Lord needs to have as a standard part of his life.

1. *You must have a willingness and desire to serve.* Where do you stand with this? Are you willing to serve? I am not just talking about in certain areas, I mean serving wherever necessary. A servant does not care who he serves. He just serves whoever is in authority. He looks at the call and the position that God has placed on an individual's life, and he starts serving.

2. *You must have the proper attitude.* This goes far beyond willingness. You can be willing to do something, but the attitude in which you do it must be acceptable.

3. *You must be willing to be held accountable.* Most people have a hard time with this one. However, you have got to accept it if you are willing to serve. You must be willing to make sure the task gets done right. This rule goes, no matter what. And, do not ever get the "I am just a volunteer" attitude, so that you can justify sloppy work.

4. *You must be diligent.* You must not stop until the work is done. The Bible says "the diligent one rules". It does not matter if you have been the last one to leave each and every service. If the task has been given to you, you must do it . . . completely.

5. *You must be willing to be submissive.* You have to be in submission to all authority in order to be an effective servant. If you are not willing to submit to someone who is over you in the leadership, then you are out of order.

6. *You must keep your commitments.* Remember, a commitment is not a commitment until it passes the test of commitment. This is the same way as knowing change is not change unless something changes. If you have committed to a department, when they are working you should be there helping.

7. *You must understand boundaries.* You must operate where God has placed you. You can not stick your nose into someone else's business, or department. Do not ever worry about what God called others to do. Just stick within your own boundaries.

8. *You must have a consistent prayer life.* Making it or missing it will depend on your prayer life. If you are not praying for your pastor, you will not flow with him. How can you reach as high as he is, when you are not hooked-up to the same source of power? If you want to be "equipped and thoroughly furnished", stay in prayer.

9. *You have to have standards in your life.* Your standards have to be God's standards. You must always think about how you project yourself. Do people around you see God in you? Are you upholding the standards of your church, of your pastor?

10. *Do not limit God.* He has given you everything that you need to do the work. He has equipped you thoroughly. He has given you everything His son and His spirit. What could be stopping you from doing the work of God?

Chapter 6

Reaching Your Fullness in God

Led by the Spirit

P rophets in the Old Testament led the people because the Holy Spirit had not yet come. Now, however, we know that the Holy Spirit guides us into all truths. The Prophets today give confirmation to what God is speaking or has spoken.

If you are actively serving, God will speak a lot of things to you. He will tell you what you need to take care of in the ministry. The pastor will be able to confirm the Word, but when you do not do the work, the Holy Spirit has to speak to the man of God directly. This is not how God wants things handled. He desires to speak directly to you.

You will never reach your fullness in God if you keep allowing your pastor to give you instructions on how to do your calling. If he is the only one hearing from God, then your ministry is hindered. You must be willing to get before God yourself. You have got to be willing to hear what God wants you to do. When you are in the right position, hearing from God directly, it will allow your pastor to go to a higher level in God. At that time, you will be able to really eat the best of God's Word.

*"Humble yourselves therefore under the mighty hand of
God, that He may exalt you in due time:"*

I PETER 5:6

Let us talk about the law of progression. Most great men of God
serve other great men of God. If you do not totally trust your pastor,
you are at the wrong church. If you can not submit to your pastor, you
are out of order.

The Word says that you should "Humble yourself." It does not
say somebody is going to humble you. When this scripture talks about
the "mighty hand of God," it is referring to all the people that He has
placed in authority. If you learn to humble yourself, He will exalt you
in due time. His Word reveals this fact. There is always a due season.
It is never "if it will happen," but, when it will happen."

Accept Small Beginnings

*"Better is the end of a thing than the beginning thereof and
the patient in spirit is better than the proud in spirit."*

ECCLESIATES 7:8

Are you more concerned about where you start, than where you
are going? Your beginnings may be small but the latter will always
be greater. This is the law of progression. It especially applies to
God's work. Many who read this book will do great things in God's
Kingdom. You must understand that you must take each step one at
a time, because your steps will be ordered by God. He may give you
the fullness of the vision up-front, but he will only give you the steps
one at a time.

In my church, I have seen a lot of people come and go because
they could not see far enough. They could not understand the "one-
step-at-a-time" process which would eventually achieve the vision.

They also could not see how their calling fit into the whole plan because they got hung-up on where they were starting. They constantly wanted to skip many steps in servanthood, without paying the price. Unfortunately, some of them bailed out too early. In essence, they sold their inheritance and were blinded by Satan because they could not understand that God uses small beginnings.

Even though you may be sweeping the floors now, you must understand that God will take you higher, if you are faithful at this level. Therefore, do not sell out. Do not lose your inheritance. It is coming. God is faithful. He will exalt you in due season.

Expect to Increase

"Though thy beginning was small, yet thy latter end should greatly increase".

JOB 8:7

Everything about God is an increase. Everything that God wants to do in your life includes an increase. God wants to increase your living. God wants to increase your giving. He wants to give you more, in every aspect of your life, much more than you could possibly imagine.

Jesus even told us this when He said we would do the "greater works". But, how can you do the "greater works?" You know that God is not a respecter of person. How can you be the one that goes higher into the things of God? By doing the work that He has called you to do, by being willing to humble yourself and submit to all authority, by doing well in your small beginnings and by being faithful over that which belongs to another man.

Finish Your Work

"So the last shall be first, and the first last: for many are called, but few are chosen."

MATTHEW 20:16

God phrased this scripture a certain way for a purpose. When you are called, you are placed last. Based on what you do in this position, determines whether you are going to be chosen to be first. In other words, if you are faithful while you are last, you'll see yourself becoming first. Few are ever chosen, because when they are called they are not faithful in their work in their small beginnings.

If you expect to do great things for God, be faithful in the small things such as where you begin your work in the Ministry of Helps. Remember, this is a part of the body that is like the pillars in the church. This is the part of the body that helps make everything run decently and in order, the way God intended it to operate. If you accept responsibility in a church department or as a P.P.A. and you do not fulfill your calling properly, you are hindering the purpose for the church. The Ministry of Helps is to support others in the church, so that they can go back out and become effective witnesses to the world.

Persecution Will Come

"Yea, and all that will live godly in Christ Jesus shall suffer persecution."

II TIMOTHY 3:12

Why do you think it is strange that you suffer persecution? After all, Jesus said that this would happen. But you have got to understand that Satan can not do anymore to you than you allow him.

We know that Satan is the god of this world. He goes about stalking the children of God. He can not devour everyone, only when someone is caught unaware. His purpose is to create distractions, to get you off your calling.

God's Word tells you what your rights are. You can choose "life or death, blessings or curses", but it will not do any good to know this truth, if you do not act on it. When you allow Satan, through his distractions, to motivate your actions, what are you choosing from God's Word?

There are two types of families on earth. There's God's family and there's Satan's family. One is activated by blessings the other moves in the curses. We know that every perfect gift comes from God. Anything else comes from Satan. Understand this is very important for every child of God. Also, understanding that Satan comes in to create distractions; not reacting to them is your key to victory.

For example, when you make a decision to tithe, what happens? You get an unexpected bill. If your pastor preaches on healing, inevitably sickness tries to come. Why? Because Satan tries to destroy the promises of God, by causing distractions. But do not ever fall for any of them, especially when it comes to you fulfilling your call. Do not ever listen to the doubts that Satan has tried to put in your mind, even while you have read this book. Remember, God says you are in control. You can either choose life or death, blessings or curses.

A lot of people speak death into their life and even on their calling. They just do not see how achieving the vision that they have on the inside of them is ever possible. They fail to realize that it is Satan who is constantly reminding them of the impossibilities. They forget that Satan attempts to clutter their memory so that they end-up getting distracted off of the promises of God. Worse yet, they forget to use their armour when Satan comes as a roaring lion.

In a teaching recently, I gave an example of how gazelles are successful at fooling the attempt of an attacking lion. In Africa, when the lion comes to stalk the gazelles, they all start bouncing around as if to show how physically fit they are. It is as if they understand that the lion always pursues the weakest one in the animal kingdom. It is amazing how many are able to escape the wiles of the lion, just by demonstrating strength in their actions.

This is what you have to do when Satan comes to kill, steal and destroy. You must put on your armour and show Satan how fit you are. You must "bounce" around with the promises of God coming out of your mouth. This is how you will overcome tribulation. When you prove yourself fit, by being filled-up with God's Word, Satan will keep moving.

Be strong in the Lord. He will help you fulfill your calling. Be fit. Bounce like a gazelle. Keep yourself filled-up with His Word, so that when Satan stalks you, he will soon find out that he can not bite through your armour. Walk in the joy of the Lord. He is your strength. Know that God has already prepared a path for you. You just need to take your first step. Get your hands busy. Start doing something in your church today. Make a final decision to become submitted and committed to your calling. Amen.

To order this book and other materials offered by
Pastor Reginald Ezell or if you would like
to become a partner of
Reginald Ezell Ministries, Inc.
you can write or call at

WORLD COVENANT CHRISTIAN
CENTER, INC.
P.O. Box 81399
Conyers, GA 30013
678-565-0378
678-565-0372 Fax

Printed in the United States
By Bookmasters